Hygiene

Jayne Denshire

Smart Apple Media
P.O. Box 3263
Mankato, MN, 56002

First published in 2010 by
MACMILLAN EDUCATION AUSTRALIA PTY LTD
15–19 Claremont St, South Yarra, Australia 3141

Visit our web site at www.macmillan.com.au or go directly to www.macmillanlibrary.com.au

Associated companies and representatives throughout the world.

Library of Congress Cataloging-in-Publication Data

Denshire, Jayne.
Hygiene / Jayne Denshire.
     p. cm. — (Healthy habits)
Includes index.
ISBN 978-1-59920-548-9 (library binding)
1. Hygiene—Juvenile literature. 2. Health—Juvenile literature. I. Title.
RA777.D39 2011
613—dc22

                        2009038470

Edited by Helena Newton
Text and cover design by Kerri Wilson
Page layout by Domenic Lauricella
Photo research by Jes Senbergs
Illustrations by Richard Morden

Manufactured in China by Macmillan Production (Asia) Ltd.
Kwun Tong, Kowloon, Hong Kong
Supplier Code: CP December 2009

Acknowledgments
The author and the publisher are grateful to the following for permission to reproduce copyright material:

Front cover photograph: Boy brushing teeth © Cristian Lazzari/iStockphoto

© Angela Hampton Picture Library/Alamy, 25 (top); © Peter Beck/Corbis, 19; © Ed Bock/Corbis, 26; Roy Morsch/Corbis, 14; © Olivia Baumgartner/Sygma/Corbis, 7 (middle); Rob Cruse, 10, 16, 17; James Darell/Getty Images, 20; Steve Lynn/Getty Images, 23; iStockphoto, 6 (top); © Jaimie Duplass/iStockphoto, 24; © Kim Gunkel/iStockphoto, 7 (bottom); © Cristian Lazzari/iStockphoto, 1, 3, 8; © Juan Monino/iStockphoto, 7 (top); © Glenda Powers/iStockphoto, 6 (bottom); Jupiter Images, 6 (middle), 21, 22; Newspix/News Ltd, 9, 25 (bottom); Photolibrary, 18; Photolibrary © Imagebroker/Alamy, 5; Photolibrary © Picture Partners/Alamy, 13, 15; Photolibrary/Debbie Boccabella, 12; Photolibrary/Tim Pannell, 11; © Monkey Business Images/Shutterstock, 4.

Contents

When a word is printed in **bold**, you can look up its meaning in the Glossary on page 31.

Healthy Habits

Healthy habits are actions we learn and understandings we develop. These actions and understandings help us be happy and healthy human beings.

Getting out in the fresh air is a healthy habit we can all learn.

If we do something often, we can carry out the action without thinking about it. This action is called a habit.

Putting on a hat every time you go out in the sun is a healthy habit.

Developing Healthy Habits

If we develop healthy habits when we are young, they become good choices for life. We can develop healthy habits in these six ways.

1 Exercise
Good exercise habits keep us fit and healthy.

2 Hygiene
Good **hygiene** habits keep us clean and healthy.

3 Nutrition
Good **nutrition** habits keep us growing and healthy.

4 Rest and sleep

Good rest and sleep habits keep us relaxed, energetic, and healthy.

5 Safety

Good safety habits keep us safe and healthy.

6 Well-being

Good **well-being** habits keep us feeling happy and healthy.

What Is Hygiene?

Hygiene is what you do to keep yourself clean and healthy. You develop hygiene habits to care for your body. This is called personal care.

Brushing your teeth twice a day is an important part of personal care.

You also develop habits to keep your home and community healthy and clean. Many of these hygiene habits help other people be healthy, too.

Collecting recycling and garbage from homes every week helps keep the community healthy.

Being Clean

Being clean means being free from most **germs**. Germs are too tiny to see. They are found in unclean places and can cause **disease**.

Germs often gather in wet areas such as bathrooms.

Germs can **infect** your body and make you unwell.
They use up your body's energy and **nutrients**.
When you clean, you get rid of germs, so they
cannot infect you.

Washing the dishes can
help get rid of germs.

Washing Your Body

Washing your body every day with soap and water will keep it clean. Soap and water remove dirt and dead skin.

Having clean skin helps keep your body free of germs.

Washing Your Hands

Washing your hands helps keep germs away. It is important to wash your hands after playing and going to the toilet. You also need to wash your hands before touching and eating food.

Washing your hands with soap and water removes more germs than washing with water alone.

Hair Care

You can care for your hair by washing, brushing, and trimming it. **Bacteria** feed on the oil in greasy hair. It is important to wash your hair regularly with shampoo.

Brushing or combing your hair every day gets rid of knots and tangles.

Head Lice and Dandruff

Head lice can breed in hair and make your **scalp** itchy. Dandruff forms when dry skin flakes off your scalp. Head lice and dandruff can be treated with special shampoos.

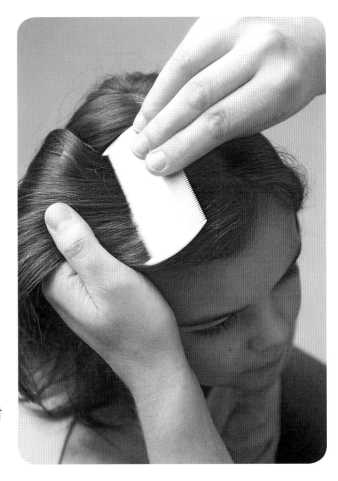

It is important for an adult to check your scalp for head lice regularly.

Nail Care

It is important to care for your nails by cleaning and trimming them regularly. You can remove the dirt from under your nails with a nail brush or nail file.

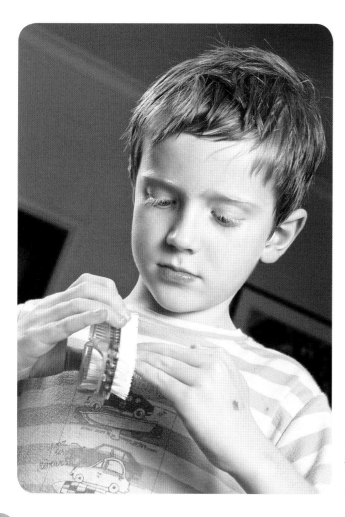

Cleaning under your fingernails helps keep germs away.

Keeping your nails short stops germs from building up under them. You can trim your nails while an adult supervises. Then use a nail file to smooth away rough edges.

Trim your nails carefully, just below the top of each finger and thumb.

Looking After Your Teeth

Looking after your teeth is important. Teeth are used to bite and chew food, so must be cleaned twice a day. Use dental floss to remove food between your teeth.

Keep your teeth clean by brushing them with a toothbrush and toothpaste twice a day.

It is important to visit the dentist regularly to check that your teeth are healthy. Your dentist will look for **tooth decay** and also check that your gums are healthy.

The dentist sometimes takes an X-ray of your teeth to look for hidden tooth decay.

Germs That Make You Sick

When harmful germs get inside your body, they can make you sick. Germs can cause illnesses, such as colds and the flu.

Colds are caused by a germ that enters your body and makes your nose run.

Good hygiene habits can stop germs from spreading.
If you have a cold:
- Cover your mouth when you cough.
- Blow your nose with tissues, and then throw the tissues away.
- Wash your hands often.

Covering your mouth when you cough can stop others from catching your cold.

Pets

Pets are great fun, but they sometimes carry germs. Washing your hands after playing with your pet can stop pet germs from spreading to you.

Try not to let your dog lick you when you are playing together.

Cleaning your pet's home or bedding regularly can help keep you and your pet healthy. Change your pet's water often, and keep the food bowl clean. Then wash your hands.

A clean food bowl will help keep your pet healthy.

People Who Help Us with Hygiene

Some people have jobs in hygiene. Nurses, dental hygienists, and podiatrists all work to help us with hygiene.

Nurses sometimes **vaccinate** children against certain diseases. School nurses also check for head lice and teach students about hygiene.

Dental hygienists work at dentists' offices. They clean teeth and remove **plaque** to help keep people's mouths healthy.

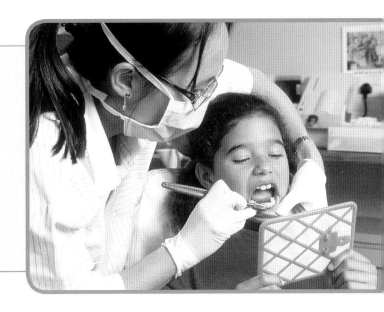

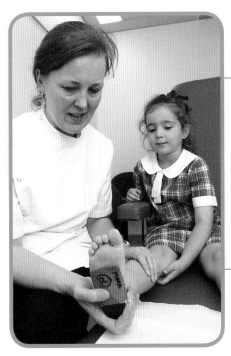

Podiatrists help keep people's feet healthy. They check that toenails are free from disease and remove unhealthy skin from the feet.

Make Hygiene a Healthy Habit

Making hygiene a healthy habit means looking after your body, your home, and your community. Good hygiene habits are important to keep you clean and healthy.

Your doctor can help you follow good hygiene habits when you are sick or hurt.

Healthy Hygiene Checklist

This checklist shows how often you should do these healthy hygiene habits.

Healthy Hygiene Habit	every day	once a week	once every two weeks	whenever it is necessary
have a bath or shower	✓			
wear clean clothes	✓			
wash your hands	✓			
brush your hair	✓			
check for head lice		✓		
cut your nails			✓	
clean your teeth	✓			
visit a dentist				✓
see a doctor				✓
clean your pet's home or bedding		✓		

Try This Healthy Habit!

You can make your own herbal shampoo, using **castile soap** and an essential oil. You can find these in health food stores and some supermarkets.

You Will Need:

- a few drops of an essential oil, such as peppermint or lavender
- 16 ounces (500 milliliters) of liquid castile soap
- a saucepan
- a wooden spoon
- a 20-ounce (600-ml) storage bottle with a removable cap
- a funnel

You can ask a parent for help.

What To Do:

1. Place a few drops of essential oil in the saucepan.

2 Add the castile soap.

3 Stir over a low heat on the stovetop until the oil and soap are blended together.

4 Allow the mixture to cool down.

5 When the mixture is cold, pour it into the storage bottle using a funnel.

6 Use your homemade herbal shampoo to wash your hair.

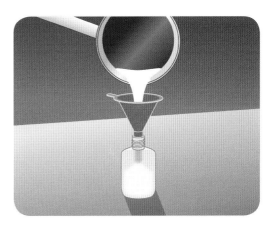

Amazing Hygiene Facts

A strand of hair grows for up to five years before it falls out. If you never cut it, it would grow to be three feet (1 meter) long.

It takes about 150 days for your fingernail to grow from your **cuticle** to your fingertip.

Teeth are alive and have blood and nerves running through them.

Your nails grow faster in summer.

Head lice cannot jump, fly, or hop. They can only get onto another head by walking along strands of hair.

Not all bacteria are unhealthy! Good bacteria live in your body, too. They help you fight infection and stay healthy.

Glossary

bacteria   tiny living things that either make plants and animals rot away or help them be healthy

castile soap   gentle soap, usually made from olive oil

cuticle   the skin that runs around the lower edge of fingernails and toenails

disease   an illness or sickness

germs   tiny living things that can cause disease

head lice   tiny insects that live, lay eggs, and feed on the scalp, making it itchy

hygiene   what we do to keep ourselves clean and healthy

infect   to spread germs or a disease

nutrients   the healthy parts of food that we need to live and grow

nutrition   what our bodies take in and use from the food we eat

plaque   a soft layer that forms on teeth and carries harmful bacteria

scalp   the skin that covers the head

tooth decay   when teeth are eaten away because plaque mixes with sugar

vaccinate   to give someone medicine or drugs to stop them from catching a disease

well-being   a state of feeling healthy and happy

Index